Forest Animals

Forest
Animals

ENCYCLOPÆDIA BRITANNICA

CHICAGO •LONDON •TORONTO •GENEVA •SYDNEY •TOKYO •MANILA •SEOUL

Advisory Board

The Treasury of American Wildlife advisory board was established to help make this book series a unique effort toward further understanding of our wildlife resources. Members come from many walks of life and share a common interest in preserving America's priceless wildlife heritage.

ISBN: 0-85229-371-2   © **1979 by Encyclopaedia Britannica, Inc.**   Printed in U.S.A.

Table of Contents

The Forest

Forests are the natural home for countless species of wildlife. Trees provide shelter and food for both birds and mammals. The forest is a safe place where wildlife can be hidden away from man and natural predators.

Pine, spruce and fir grow in the boreal forest of the North, stretching from Alaska across Canada. These *conifers* keep their needles all year round and are well suited to cold temperatures. So are the timber wolf, wolverine, porcupine and other animals that live there.

The northern hardwood/coniferous forest extends from the upper Great Lakes through New England. Here leaf-bearing deciduous trees such as oak, maple, beech, birch and hemlock mix with the pines. Deer, bear and turkey make their home here.

In the eastern *deciduous* forest, cherry, walnut and hickory grow with oak, maples and pines. Gray squirrels chatter in the treetops while bears, raccoons and opossums live on the forest floor.

Mountain sheep and goats, elk and cougar thrive in the deep forests of the Rocky Mountains.

As a forest grows, it also changes. Trees that have one set of light, heat and moisture needs may die out and new ones come in. As the forest changes, so does the wildlife population that lives there.

America's Forests

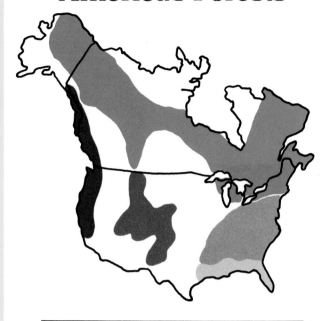

■ **Northern Boreal Forest**
■ **Northern Hardwood and Conifer Forest**
■ **Eastern Deciduous Forest**
■ **Southern Evergreen Forest**
■ **Rocky Mountain Forest**
■ **Pacific Rain Forest**

Brush

Forest Glades

Timber Wolf

The northern forest is home to the few timber wolves which remain. The howl of the wolf is a haunting sound of the North.

Wild Turkey

Though wild turkeys live in the hardwood forests, they depend on forest clearings to find food and raise young.

Deer

The white-tailed deer prefers the hardwood forest. It eats acorns and other nuts, as well as buds and twigs called "browse."

Soft and Hardwood

Second Growth

Conifer

Ruffed Grouse

Ruffed grouse live in brushy thickets. If a person comes too close for comfort the bird takes off in an explosive flurry of wings.

Gray Squirrel

The squirrel lives in the tallest trees of the forest. Nut trees provide its favorite food.

Black Bear

The dense, mature forest is the home of the black bear. Bears like nuts and berries for food.

Opossum

The opossum lives near the edge of the forest. It eats insects, eggs, berries and what it can steal from gardens.

Elk

The elk lives in western forests and meadows. It is a herd animal and can be seen most often at dawn and dusk.

The Timber Wolf

Many years ago, the timber, or gray, wolf lived throughout most of North America. Today, only a few small packs of timber wolves live in Mexico. A great many survive in remote parts of Canada and Alaska. But the call of the timber wolf is a rare sound in the lower 48 states.

As farming and cattle raising grew in the United States, buffalo and other game animals were destroyed. The wolf depended on these animals for food. It was forced to adjust by eating smaller animals, such as rabbits and mice, and by hunting sheep and cattle.

To a wolf, killing a farm animal is no different from hunting an elk or a moose. But people would not allow the wolves to kill their livestock. Suddenly the hunter became the hunted. People killed huge numbers of timber wolves with traps and poisons. They offered payments called bounties for wolf skins. Humans have even hunted wolves by shooting them from low-flying airplanes.

Like other predators, wolves usually hunt and kill the old, stray, young or sick animals in a herd. This is nature's way and helps to insure that the fittest, healthiest animals in the herd survive and reproduce.

A year in the life of a young wolf

Wolves grow up in a hurry. When born in March or April, pups weigh about a pound (454 grams) each. They are born deaf, blind and helpless. In 10 to 14 days, their eyes open. By their second month they are exploring the world outside the den, and as summer turns to fall, the pups are nearly full grown. Seven years is the average life span of a wolf, though some live as long as 12 to 14 years in their forest home.

Summer
Pups stop nursing at about six weeks and learn to eat meat. They are very playful at this age.

Spring
Four to six pups are born in March or April.

Fall
Pups are nearly full grown and weigh about 60 pounds.

Winter
The pups become part of the pack. Older brothers and sisters rejoin the group for the winter season when food is hard to find.

Wolves help keep nature in balance

Wolves eat a wide variety of animals and birds. They thrive on rabbits and other plentiful small game.

Populations of deer, moose and caribou are kept under control by wolves. At one time, the Isle Royale moose herd numbered 3,000, far more than the island could support. Many of the moose starved. After the wolves were introduced, the moose herd gradually was reduced to the number the island could feed.

The number of wolves at Isle Royale has stabilized, too. A moose's hooves and antlers are dangerous, and sometimes wolves are killed as the pack closes in for the kill.

A relatively small number of wolves can control a large animal population. A wolf may eat 20 pounds (10 kilograms) of meat at one time. One moose provides enough meat to feed a pack for only two or three days. Then the pack must move out to find more food in the forest.

Wolves live in packs

Wolves live and hunt in packs averaging about 12 animals. The wolf pack usually is a related family. It is made up of the mother and father, plus their one- and two-year-old offspring. Sometimes two families will band together, but usually there is some kinship. Aunts, uncles and cousins all live and hunt together in harmony.

The whole group must work together to kill a large animal like a moose. In a night of hunting, the pack often travels 25 to 50 miles (40 to 80 kilometers) in a huge circle. They signal to each other by howling.

There is one leader for the pack. He is the strongest male. The leader controls the others with barks and growls and just by the angle of his head and tail. Every action of the leader means something to the individual members of the wolf pack.

What do wolves look like?

Wolves are many different shades of color. Those living in the Arctic are nearly white. Others in our northern forests may be gray or almost black.

The white wolves of the Arctic are the largest. Some are more than seven feet (two meters) long from nose to tip of tail. They weigh as much as 175 pounds (80 kilograms). Other wolves are about the size of big dogs and resemble the German Shepherd.

Wolves are intelligent and playful. They nuzzle each other and wag their tails when they meet friends. They are very loyal to the family and the pack with which they travel and hunt for food animals.

Where do wolves live?

Wolves are adaptable and can live under many different conditions. When this country was young, wolves were found throughout our forests, on the Great Plains, near deserts and even along the seashore. Now they have retreated to the few remaining wilderness areas of the United States and Canada. Wolves seek the remote forest to be as far away from human predators as possible. There they can find the wild animals they prefer to eat.

Today, there are several dozen wolves at Isle Royale National Park, an island in Lake Superior. Here, scientists are studying the relationship between wolves and moose. Other small packs live in northern Michigan, Minnesota and Wisconsin. A large population can be found in Algonquin Provincial Park in Canada. A few packs stray back and forth between Canada and the U.S. in Glacier National Park.

Alaska has more wolves by far than any other state. Still, numbers are surprisingly small. In one count, there were only 115 wolves in a 7,000 square mile (18,100 square kilometer) area. And this was in a section where there is an abundance of moose, a favorite food.

TIMBER WOLF FACTS

Habitat: Wilderness forests and tundra.

Habits: Live in packs. Each wolf knows its social standing in pack. Young are born in a den. Requires 10 square miles (26 square kilometers) per wolf.

Food: Woodland caribou, moose, white-tailed deer, beaver, smaller animals such as rabbits and mice.

Size and Weight: Up to seven feet (two meters) long, including tail; up to 175 pounds (80 kilograms).

Life Span: Seven years average, some to 14.

Locomotion: Thirty-five to 40 miles per hour (56-64 kilometers), can broad jump at least 12 feet (3.7 meters).

Voice: Howling, growling, barking and whimpering.

The Wild Turkey

When Thanksgiving Day is mentioned, most Americans think of turkey. But the bird the Pilgrims feasted on at the first thanksgiving celebration was not our native wild turkey. The Pilgrims ate gobblers they had brought with them from England, not knowing that larger, wild turkeys were common in the woodlands around Plymouth, Massachusetts.

Wild turkeys are similar in many ways to the common barnyard varieties. The males are called toms, cocks or gobblers. Their gobbling sounds the same in the forest or on the farm. The hens are generally smaller than the toms. In the wild, turkeys are shy and hard to get close to. They have strong wings and fly swiftly. But when frightened, they prefer to run, some as fast as 25 miles per hour (40 kilometers).

Turkeys spend their days on the ground, searching for acorns, dried fruit and other nuts and berries. At night the birds sleep in the upper branches of trees, where they are much safer from enemies.

When a flock is feeding, one or more birds are alert and watching for danger. Foxes, badgers, coyotes, skunks—these and other predators—pose a constant threat to wild turkeys and their young.

Toms spend their winter together in flocks away from the hens and young. In spring, the old toms leave the flocks to attract hens. When courting, the male spreads his beautiful big bronze tail into a fan and struts before a hen.

A bird with history

The turkey the Pilgrims ate on their first Thanksgiving was a descendant of the Mexican turkey, which was brought from Mexico to Europe by Spanish explorers. From Spain the bird was taken to England and arrived in our country with the English colonists. Many Mexican turkeys were shipped to England through the Turkish Empire. Some believe this is how the bird got its name. In England, it was called a "turkie fowle."

To Benjamin Franklin, the native turkey was the "all-American" bird. He tried to have Congress name it our national symbol, but Congress preferred the bald eagle.

Native American children often hunted turkeys for food, clothing and for feathers to put on arrows. A boy disguised in a turkey skin hid behind a log, showed some feathers and called like a turkey. If the bird came close enough, the boy caught it with his hands.

A primitive lifestyle

After mating, a hen turkey goes alone to make her nest. She scratches a hollow in dead leaves, usually under a bush or log. There she lays eight to 15 light brown eggs peppered with reddish-brown spots and dots. The hen sits on the eggs for 28 days before they hatch. When she leaves her nest to feed, she picks up dried leaves with her bill and covers the eggs to hide them from foxes, skunks and other enemies and keep them warm. If the eggs are destroyed a second nest may be started. When the eggs hatch, the baby turkeys, called "poults," come into the world with eyes open and bodies covered with wet down. Within a few hours the little ones are dry and able to follow their mother away from the nest, never to return.

The mother alone cares for the young, raising one family a year. She protects them from enemies and keeps them dry. If chilled, a young turkey may die quickly, so the young sleep or "roost" beneath their mother's wings until they are several weeks old.

The turkey population can vary greatly from one year to the next. A cold or wet nesting season can wipe out huge numbers of young turkeys. If undisturbed, however, the birds may live for 10 or 12 years.

The turkey survives

The great numbers of wild turkeys that roamed the forests of the eastern and central United States began to disappear rapidly after the settlers arrived. The big birds were killed for food, and the clearing of forests destroyed their native habitat.

In Massachusetts, the last wild turkey was seen in 1851. By 1930 the birds were scarce everywhere. A great and united effort by game managers brought them back. The release of farm-raised birds in the wild, strict management of hunting and improvement of woodlands have all helped to stop the decline. Today, there are more wild turkeys in most eastern and southern states than even before the colonists came.

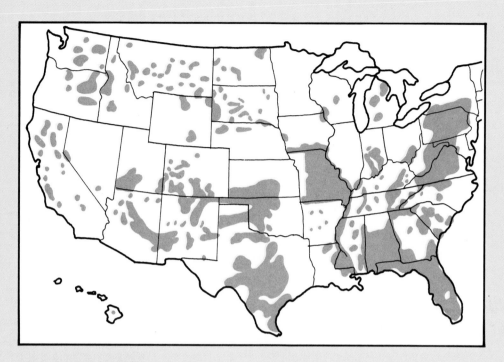

WILD TURKEY FACTS

Habitat: Forest and woodland clearings, mostly in hilly or mountainous regions.

Habits: Males spend winters in flocks away from hens and young. In spring, toms may attract many hens by displaying and gobbling.

Food: Principally mast such as acorns, grapes, beechnuts, wild cherry and dried nuts and fruits found on ground.

Size and Weight: A streamlined version of the familiar barnyard turkey. Males, 48 inches (122 centimeters) long, 15-20 pounds (seven-nine kilograms); females, 34 inches (86 centimeters) long, about nine pounds (four kilograms).

Life Span: Undisturbed may live 10-12 years. Few do because of hunting pressure.

Locomotion: Have strong wings and can fly swiftly. Run as fast as 25 miles an hour (40 kilometers).

Voice: Similar to "gobbling" of domestic turkey; call sounds like "took, took, took."

The White-tailed Deer

A deer is many things to many people. To the hunter, it is the smartest and most desirable game animal in the forest. To the farmer, it is a nuisance that eats his crops. To the motorist driving in deer country, it is a possible hazard at every turn of the road.

The white-tailed deer is at home in northern and southern forests. There it finds lots of twigs and buds, called "browse," to eat. Deer also locate food by digging under leaves and snow with their sharp hooves. A deer's hooves are really more like toenails than feet. Prehistoric deer had five toes on each foot, as we have. But over the passage of time the animals have changed. Modern deer grow two long, sharp toenails, aids in running and digging. Two smaller, useless toes grow on each leg, up above the foot.

Deer have very good eyes, noses and ears. But deer are color blind. That is why hunters can wear bright red or orange clothing for safety and still not be seen by deer. The slightest movement or noise, however, will alert the deer. When alarmed, it raises its white tail as a signal to other deer and bounds away.

A year in the life of a deer

Spring is fawning time in the forest, when females, or does, give birth to their fawns in protected thickets or tall, grassy fields.

One-year-old deer are known as yearlings. A yearling doe will usually have only one fawn. But older does may have twins, triplets or even quadruplets.

As soon as a fawn is born, it gets its first bath...a thorough cleaning, from head to hoof, by its mother's rough tongue.

The fawn nurses like a calf or a colt, punching and pulling at its mother's udder and wagging its tiny white tail as it sucks. Does' milk is very rich and contains much more protein and butterfat than the best cows' milk.

Within an hour after birth, the doe leads her wobbly-legged youngster to a better hiding place, where coyotes, bobcats, cougars and dogs are less likely to find it. Until it is about a week old, the fawn remains curled up and hidden on the forest floor. Its spotted coat keeps it well camouflaged, and during those first few days it has little or no smell to attract enemies.

The fawn grows rapidly on its mother's milk. At about three weeks old, it can run faster than a man. Its mother then takes the youngster with

her as she searches for food in the forest. The fawn soon begins to nibble at tender twigs and grasses.

By September, the fawn is nearly full grown. Not only is it eating like an adult, but it has lost its spots. If it is a male, or buck, it will grow little knobs, called buttons, on its head. Only its baby face and small size show that it is still a youngster.

Fawns remain with their mothers through their first winter, following and sometimes even leading the small band of does, fawns and bucks which live within about one square mile (1.6 square kilometers) of forest, their home territory. The first winter may be the hardest for the fawns. When thick ice and snow cover their food on the ground, their short necks and legs do not allow them to reach as high as the adults for browse in trees.

When spring comes, however, deer regain their strength quickly as they eat the first green growth. It is fawning time again. Does, now heavy with twin fawns, drive away their youngsters of the year before. The bewildered creatures are on their own.

All about antlers

During the spring, yearling bucks start to grow their first set of real antlers. Depending on the vitamins and minerals in their diet, the antlers will be at least "spikes," like two nails sticking out the top of their head. Older bucks who have eaten well will grow six, eight, 10 or even 12 points, or branches, off the main antler. Usually half the points grow on one antler and half on the other. The number of points does not tell how old a buck is.

In early summer, the antlers are soft and covered with a brown fuzz called "velvet." But as the breeding season approaches, the antlers become hard and the deer rubs the velvet off against small trees. You know there is a buck in the forest when you see a tree that

has a fresh "buck rub."

In the autumn, bucks use their antlers to fight other bucks for the attention of the does and to claim territory. But when the "rut," or breeding season, is over in late autumn, the antlers are no longer needed. They drop off between December and February.

As winter approaches, deer change in other ways, too. Their rusty red summer coats are shed for thicker and darker winter coats. Deer hairs are hollow, and air trapped in each hair helps keep the deer warm on even the coldest days. Native Americans used buckskins, with the hair left on, as winter clothing. Some pioneers also found buckskin practical.

White-tailed deer live nearby

If you live in or near a forest, the chances are pretty good that you see deer regularly. White-tailed deer can be found in all 48 lower states, all provinces of southern Canada and in northern Mexico. The estimate of 12½ million white-tailed deer in the United States today is many times the number that were here when the Pilgrims landed at Plymouth. The new growth that resulted from the clearing of forests created more browse for the deer to eat.

The other common deer in North America is called the mule deer. It has a black tip on its tail, larger ears and slightly different antlers. There are fewer mule deer than white-tailed deer, and they are found only in the West.

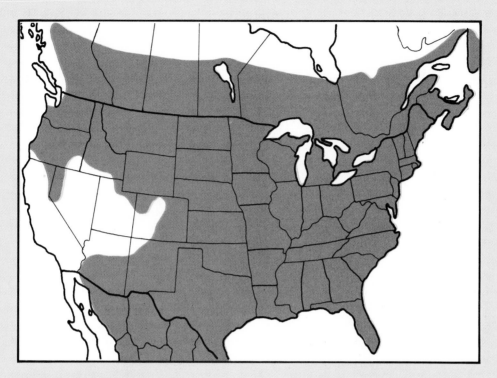

WHITE-TAILED DEER

Habitat: Forest and clearings.

Habits: Most active in early morning and late evening.

Size and Weight: Most weigh around 100 pounds (45 kilograms), but they can weigh up to 400 pounds (180 kilograms). They are about 3-3½ feet (one meter) tall at the shoulder.

Life Span: Though most live only 1½ years, they can live 16½ years in the wild.

Locomotion: Runs 35-40 miles per hour (55-65 kilometers); can jump 8½ feet (2.5 meters) high and 30 feet (nine meters) across.

Voice: Light blat, rarely heard. Snorts when alarmed. Fawns bleat.

The Ruffed Grouse

The ruffed grouse is related to the prairie chicken, ptarmigan and other kinds of grouse. In the South, some folks call it a "pheasant." In the North, it is known as a "partridge." To early settlers it was a "wood hen," a rather tame creature that sat quietly on tree limbs even when approached by humans. Pioneer hunters did a thriving business knocking grouse out of trees with sticks and bringing the delicious meat to market.

Farming gradually destroyed much of the woodland where grouse lived. But today the bird is prospering as a result of reforestation and strict controls on hunting.

The ruffed grouse today is not nearly so tolerant of humans as its ancestors. Though the young birds are fairly tame, the mature ruffed grouse is one of America's most prized game birds.

The forest provides food and shelter for the ruffed grouse. In summer berries from low growing bushes are a favorite food. The birds also like wild grapes and apples. Acorns from oak trees feed the grouse in fall months. During the winter the grouse finds shelter in deep forest where it can find aspen and birch buds to eat.

The call of the drum

In spring, members of the grouse family woo their mates with elaborate dances and noises—hoots, booms, drummings, coos, struts, puffs and toots. The ruffed grouse is a drummer. He performs his amazing act usually in the morning and evening on logs or rocks in his territory. Tail flattened against the drumming perch, the male beats his wings forward and upward to produce a drumming sound several times a day. Actual performances last only about eight seconds. The noise carries far. At a distance, the slow "thump, thump, thumping" gets louder and faster, ending in a whirr. The male drums to attract females, or hens, and to warn males to keep away.

At home in the forest

Lured by the males' drumming, hens come to the area to mate. Afterward they may never see their mates again. The duties of raising the young are the hen's alone. She builds a nest at the base of a tree or stump, or under a log or rock. The hen scratches out a shallow bowl. There she lays nine to 12 light brown eggs, some speckled with darker brown spots.

She sits on them from 21 to 24 days, until they hatch.

As soon as the downy, newly hatched chicks are dry, the hen leads them away from the nest. If danger approaches, she warns her babies with a sharp call, and they scurry to cover under leaves and twigs. To lure a fox or other enemy away from the young, the mother grouse pretends to have a broken wing.

The artful dodger

One of the great thrills for hunters and birdwatchers alike is to surprise and flush a ruffed grouse from its hiding place. Almost underfoot, the bird explodes in a roar of wings. Before a hunter can realize what's happened, the bird is up and away over the treetops. The grouse's color and marking blend with its surroundings. It takes a top-notch grouse hunter to hit one bird out of three.

A grouse can also fly away in silence if it chooses. The sudden explosion seems designed to do just what it does—scare the dangerous intruder away.

How the grouse survives

Ruffed grouse do not migrate. If undisturbed, they may live in one suitable woodland for their entire lives. In autumn, grouse feast on wild grapes, apples and dogwood fruits. Acorns also are eaten when they are in good supply. Berries form a large part of the birds' diet. This fact has created a strange condition known as "crazy flight." Overripe berries, or those that have frozen and then thawed, may begin to ferment. Grouse, drunk or high on fermented berries, sometimes break their necks by flying against houses and into windows.

Winter is often hard for the grouse. Since most members of this family live in the North, where winters are cold and snowy, they have learned to survive where other birds might not. Grouse find shelter among evergreen trees in deep forests and feed on aspen and birch buds. They grow comblike bristles on the sides of their toes, which act as snowshoes. During storms, grouse dig into snowbanks for protection.

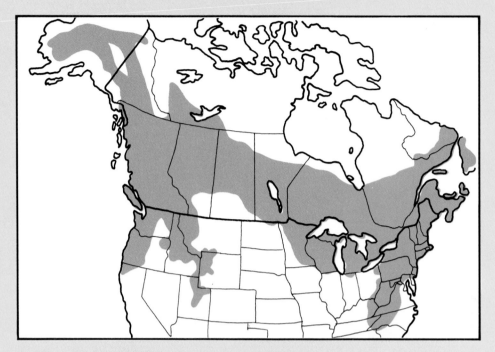

RUFFED GROUSE FACTS

Habitat: Forested areas of mature trees and/or bushy thickets.

Habits: Remains on home ground all its life. Solitary in winter, but in spring males move into area with suitable drumming logs where they attract females. Males mate with a number of females and have no domestic duties.

Food: In winter, buds and twigs; also grapes and berries. In summer, fruits, berries, seeds, catkins, some insects.

Size: Adults 16-19 inches (41-48 centimeters) long. Females have shorter tails.

Life Span: About six years.

Locomotion: Usually takes off with loud whirring of wings; can flush noiselessly. Walks with easy, graceful steps.

Voice: Alarm note is "quit-quit." Female with young will whine when surprised. Male's spring drumming sounds like a muffled "thump, thump, thump," with thumps getting louder and faster.

Watch for grouse near you

Any fair-sized woodlot, especially on a farm, may shelter this lovely game bird. Grouse may be found at any time of year in their home surroundings, but in spring you can be sure they are present if you hear the male drumming. Try to find the log or rock from which he beats his message. The log may be well worn and covered with fresh droppings.

The Gray Squirrel

A forest isn't complete without gray squirrels scurrying in the dry leaves, racing through the tops of big trees, cracking nuts loudly, or scolding anyone or anything they choose. Gray squirrels prefer forests of mature oak, beech, cherry, walnut, hickory and maple trees. They are also at home in city parks and backyards, where they may be the only wildlife, other than birds, that can be seen in the city.

If you have a feeding station for birds in your yard, you probably have gray squirrels eating there, too. Some people don't like squirrels and try to discourage them with "squirrel-proof" bird feeders. Other people enjoy watching the antics of the bushytails as much as watching birds.

In autumn, gray squirrels spend much of the day gathering and burying a variety of nuts called "mast." Later in the winter, when food is scarce, squirrels use their excellent sense of smell to find the buried nuts under a deep coat of snow.

Gray squirrels, as their name tells us, are usually gray. But sometimes they are pure white or jet black. In Olney, Illinois, several hundred rare, all-white albino squirrels are the town's trademark. They are protected by city law. Black/gray squirrels are usually found in the most northern part of the gray squirrel's range. Both black-colored and gray-colored gray squirrels can be born in the same litter.

A squirrel's first year

Female squirrels have litters twice each year. The young are born either in late winter or late summer. The mother gives birth—usually to triplets—in a tree cavity or in a leafy nest anchored in the branches of a tree. In the winter, when the trees are bare, the leaf nests can easily be seen.

At birth, the tiny squirrels have no hair, and their eyes and ears are sealed shut. They leave the nest for the first time after about six weeks to explore nearby branches and nibble on tender leaves and buds. At two months, their teeth and jaws are strong enough to crack even the hardest hickory nuts and acorns. Shortly afterward, the young squirrels are able to take care of themselves, and they leave their mother. When they are about 10 months old, they are grown and on their own.

Top-notch tree planter

Have you ever looked at an oak or walnut tree that was growing where there were no others like it and wondered how it got there? Maybe it had a little help from a squirrel. Because squirrels never recover all the nuts they bury, many that are left in the ground sprout and become trees.

Squirrels have an amazing ability to climb, jump and keep their balance on small branches. This picture shows a bold squirrel hanging from his hind legs as he gets a meal from a bird feeder.

The family of squirrels

There are about 40 different kinds of squirrels in North America. The colorful fox squirrel, with its tawny or reddish fur, and the smaller red or pine squirrels are closely related to the gray squirrel. The three cousins have similar lifestyles. But other members of the squirrel family are quite different. The thirteen-lined ground squirrel (gopher) and the chipmunk both hibernate in underground dens during the winter. The flying squirrel is the only nocturnal member of the squirrel family. That is, it sleeps during the day and is active at night. Though it doesn't really fly, this tiny squirrel can glide 150 feet (50 meters) or more through the air with the help of loose folds of skin between its legs. The forest is an ideal home for squirrels.

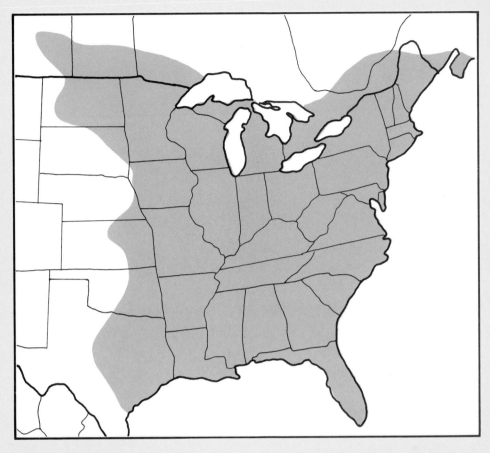

GRAY SQUIRREL FACTS

Habitat: Wooded areas with nut trees.

Habits: Active all day, all year. Seldom far from trees.

Food: Wild nuts, mushrooms, seeds and buds and, occasionally, birds' eggs and young
animal bones and antlers.

Size and Weight: Adults weigh between 1-1½ pounds (454-680 grams) and are 18-20
inches (46-51 centimeters) long.

Life Span: Average in the wild is only one year, but have been known to live nine years.
In captivity, 15-20 years is possible.

Locomotion: Scurries along the ground at about 12 miles per hour (19 kilometers).
Travels easily from tree to tree by jumping.

Voice: Various scolding, barking and chucking noises.

The Black Bear

We know less about the private lives of wild bears than we know about most other creatures of the forest. Until very recently, we didn't know how to tell the age of a bear. Scientists finally realized that they could pull a bear's tooth, cut it across and count the growth rings—just the way we tell the age of a tree.

Here are some other things that we know. Of the four kinds of bears in North America—black, grizzly, polar and brown—the black is the smallest, most common and most mild-tempered. Nevertheless, all bears, including the blacks, are dangerous wild animals and have been known to kill people.

Black bears live wherever there are deep forests. Some species make their home in the Gulf states. Others are found in the North including Canada and Alaska. The Rocky Mountains are another favorite home of the black bear.

Bears like the food provided by the trees of the forest. They eat fruits, nuts and berries along with leaves and buds. The bear isn't very fussy about his diet. He also likes honey, fish, eggs, small animals and garbage dumped by man.

The winter sleep

The bear's winter sleep has fascinated humans for generations. The bear is not a true hibernator like woodchucks, chipmunks and many reptiles. Its body temperature drops only four degrees while it sleeps, not six degrees like true hibernators. Bears do not drink or eat during this one- to four-month period, yet they awaken in March or April in good health.

A cub's first year

Bear cubs are born in late January or early February during the female's, or sow's, winter sleep. Two cubs is the usual number, though there are sometimes as many as five in a litter. They weigh only ⅛ ounce (four grams) at birth and are blind, toothless and have almost no hair. When they leave the winter den with their mother in early spring, they are two months old and already weigh about five pounds (two kilograms). During the summer they grow rapidly, and by November, when they go back to their winter den to sleep, they will weigh as much as 55 pounds (25 kilograms).

One of the first things that a mother black bear teaches her cubs is to climb up the nearest tree when there is danger. They must stay there, even if it takes many hours, until she gives the all-clear signal. Mother bear communicates with her cubs by growling, woofing and making other noises from deep within her throat. Cubs usually stay with their mother through their second summer, living in the same den or one nearby.

Black bears also talk to each other by clawing trees. Though scientists are not sure, they think these scratches are made by the male, or boar, with his 1¼ inch (three centimeter) claws to signal other bears to keep out of his five to 15 square mile (13 to 39 square kilometer) territory.

Bears can be too friendly

Black bears in the wild are among the shyest of all animals. But some of the bears in our national parks have learned that they can get an easy meal from people who have come to the park to see them. Foolish people ignore the "Don't Feed the Bears" signs and walk right up to the big, furry creatures. The more people feed the bears, the more the bears expect to be fed. Many people are injured, and some even killed, by bears who are looking for a handout. Don't violate the law by feeding the bears and adding to the dangerous problem.

The friendly, gentle bears you see on TV have long training and even they aren't really safe. Never take a chance with a wild bear.

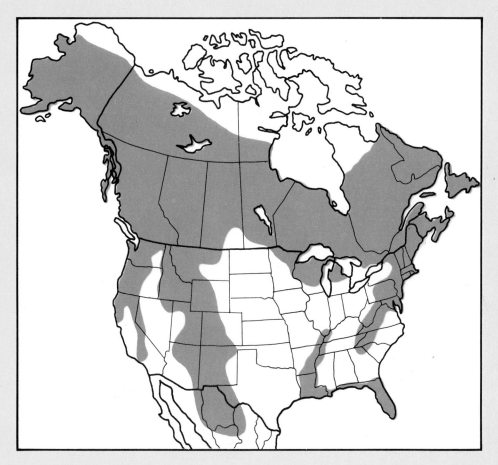

BLACK BEAR FACTS

Habitat: Forests and swamps.

Habits: Active mostly at night. Spends winter sleeping.

Food: Fruits, berries, nuts, insects, leaves and buds, honey, fish, some eggs and small animals.

Size and Weight: Adults weigh from 100-600 pounds (45-270 kilograms); are about six feet (two meters) long from head to tail.

Life Span: Can live 25 years, but the average is 12-15 years.

Locomotion: Bears amble along with a flat-foot walk, but are capable of running 30 miles per hour (50 kilometers). Good climbers.

Voice: Mothers and cubs communicate by various whimpers.

The Opossum

Imagine an animal whose hind feet look like hands and that uses its tail as a hand; whose appearance hasn't changed much since its ancestors roamed among the dinosaurs a million years ago. Imagine a distant cousin of the kangaroo. All these will help you picture the opossum.

The opossum is not handsome. Its face is long with a round pink nose like a pig's. Its 50 teeth are long and pointed. The animal has dark, beady eyes. Its tail and toes are pink and bare. The opossum looks like a cat-sized rat at first glance. Its fur has a soft undercoat covered by longer, coarser fur. The animal blends easily with its surroundings.

The southern states are the favorite home of the opossum. They also are found in the North and along the Pacific coast.

These animals usually live along the edge of the forest. They eat frogs, snakes, lizards and other small animals of the wild. However, they have grown fond of food provided by man. They share his garden, his berry patch and his eggs. Sweet corn is the animal's favorite food. The opossum also likes to raid garbage cans.

Why does it survive?

The opossum does not have a large brain. It does not have a tough hide. Nor does it run very fast. Then why has it survived for millions of years when dinosaurs, mastodons, passenger pigeons, Carolina parakeets and many others have not? The answer has several parts.

Its fur is not as popular for clothes as that of other more beautiful animals. Second, the opossum has an unusual defense against predators. When it is cornered, it "plays dead." It flops limply on its side with eyes closed and tongue hanging out. Dogs are reported to leave an opossum like this alone. Its unpleasant odor may also protect it from foxes, owls and other animals hunting for food.

An opossum is a marsupial

A real clue to the survival of these animals may be in the number of young they have and the way the young grow. A female opossum has a litter of from five to 18 young, once a year in the North, and twice a year in the South. At birth an opossum baby is smooth, pink and hairless. Its hind legs are not fully grown, and its eyes are not yet open. It is smaller than a honeybee. Although it cannot walk, it can wriggle and claw its way to a pocket formed in the skin on the underside of its mother's body. An animal that carries its young in a pouch like this is called a marsupial. The opossum is the only marsupial in North America.

The young feed on their mother's milk for their first two months. The female's nipples, usually 13, are hidden inside her pocket. If there are more babies than nipples, the last to arrive will die, for they cannot get food. But those who do get food are well protected.

In the mother's pouch a young opossum develops its legs fully. Its eyes develop and open. A coat of fine fur protects it when it ventures out. By this time it is about the size of a full-grown mouse. For the next month or so the litter stays close to the mother, sometimes riding on her back.

51

Special features

An opossum's tail is prehensile, which means "capable of grasping." Fingers are prehensile. So are some monkeys' tails. The opossum's prehensile tail helps in climbing down trees and getting into hard-to-reach places. The tail is used also to carry material for lining the den. The female can hold her tail forward over her back so several of her young can hang on it by their own tails as they travel.

Oddly, it is not the front feet but the hind feet of a 'possum that look like hands and can grasp branches. The "thumb" has no claw, as do all the other toes.

How opossums spend their days and nights

The 'possum spends most days quietly. Usually it sleeps in a hollow tree or log or in a hole under rocks or a building— any place dry and warm. At night, or on dark and gloomy

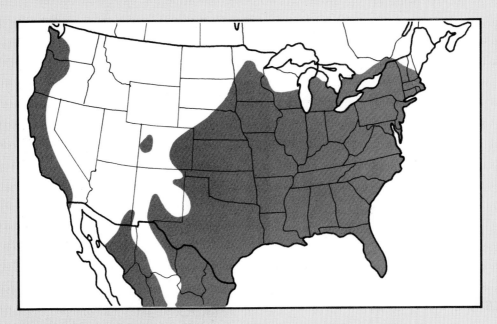

OPOSSUM FACTS

Habitat: Forests, woodlands and farmlands.

Habits: Active at night; very adaptable.

Foods: Carrion, insects, mice, frogs, snakes, lizards, eggs, fruits, berries and garbage. Especially fond of corn, persimmons, pokeberries.

Size and Weight: Total 24-34 inches (60-86 centimeters) long; tail 10-13 inches (25-33 centimeters); 5½-7 inches (14-18 centimeters) high at shoulder; 4-14 pounds (two-six kilograms).

Life Span: About two years, seven in captivity.

Locomotion: Walks, runs slowly, climbs well.

Voice: A rare growl, bark or moan; during courtship a clicking of teeth and tongue. Hisses when threatened.

days, it roams the 15 or more acres (six hectares) where it chooses to live. Here it hunts a variety of small animals, eggs, insects, fruits and berries. It has been known to search through garbage cans and steal from your gardens. The opossum is especially fond of corn.

The 'possum travels alone except for mothers with babies, and it may be out in cold weather. If the weather is very bad, it may stay in its den without food for several days at a time.

It is surprising how seldom 'possums are sighted, considering how many of them there are. Because it travels at night and its coloring blends with its surroundings, you'll have to look hard to spot a 'possum.

The Elk

One of the most exciting sounds of a Rocky Mountain forest is the bugling of the great bull elk and the crashing of their antlers as they battle for females, or cows. These battles take place as the elk slowly make their way down from the high country to their wintering grounds. The fighting is fierce and can be fatal if an elk is slashed by his opponent's sharp antlers. Elk are polygamous—one bull will mate with many cows during the rutting season. In September and October, a powerful fighter may collect a harem of 30 or more cows with their calves.

A herd of migrating elk is a dramatic sight. Many people consider them the most handsome and graceful members of the deer family. No deer has more beautiful antlers. The elk's summer coat is tawny. The legs and mane are slightly darker than the rest of the animal, while the rump and tail are pale yellow. In winter the coat is darker, grayer and heavier. Newborn calves are light tan with dull white spots, which disappear by the time they are about four months old. The Shawnee name for elk, "wapiti," means "light-colored deer." The pale rump and tail are the chief identifying features of elk, young or old, in any season.

Elk retreated west

When white people first came to North America, about 10 million elk roamed the forests and plains from coast to coast, and from Mexico into Canada. But much of their habitat was destroyed. They could not live with people and fences. Today, most of the herds are found in the Rocky Mountains and in mountains along the Pacific Coast. The evergreen forests of the West provide food and safe places for the young to be born and grow.

SUMMER RANGE

Though elk are both browsers, eating buds, leaves and young shoots of bushes and trees, and grazers, eating grasses and herbs, they prefer grazing. The high mountain meadows where the elk spend the warm months provide lush grass. By late summer the animals are sleek and plump, ready for the battles and hard winter ahead.

WINTER RANGE

In the past, after the first heavy snow, elk migrated over the same paths year after year to lower areas where food was easier to find. They still migrate, but old routes have been broken up by campgrounds, resorts, ranches and fences. One of the best-known wintering areas is the 24,000 acre (10,000 hectare) National Elk Refuge in Jackson Hole, Wyoming. Tens of thousands of elk gather there. They are fed great amounts of hay in a program financed by state and federal governments. However, the conflict between people and animals for land, and the overpopulation of elk on the land available to them, are still unsolved problems.

The elk calf

Most calves are born in May or June, usually one calf to a cow. Minutes after its birth, a calf sucks milk from its mother and tries a few awkward steps, but it soon hides in the thicket where it was born. The calf lies as quietly as if it were dead.

From time to time its mother returns so it can have more milk. After a week it runs about and eats a bit of grass. By the end of summer it can find food for itself, but it returns to its mother for milk until well into the cold winter months.

The great antlers

Each winter the antlers of elk bulls break off close to the skull, just like those of the white-tailed deer. The first knobs of new antlers appear in March or April. As they develop, they are soft, filled with blood and covered with "velvet," like deer antlers. The bulls get thin and cranky while their antlers are growing and go off by themselves. When the new antlers are fully grown and hard, the bulls rub against trees and shrubs to brush off the "velvet." Each year the new antlers of a healthy bull are larger than the previous set. By September, the many-pronged rack is long, hard and sharp, and ready for battle. A mature bull's antlers may be as wide as his height.

An animal of stature

The elk is the largest member of the deer family in North America except the moose. A newborn elk weighs 25 to 40 pounds (12 to 18 kilograms), as much as a three- or four-year-old child. It takes four years for an elk to reach full size.

Mature cows are about three-fourths the size of bulls. Like most females of the deer family, they do not have antlers. A cow is able to be bred when she is about 1½ years old. A bull can breed at one year, but does not, because he cannot gather a harem of cows until he is bigger and stronger. A full-grown male may be 9½ feet (2¾ meters) long, five feet (1½ meters) high at the shoulder and weigh more than 750 pounds (350 kilograms).

They live in herds

Throughout the year, elk are sociable creatures. But the make-up of the herd shifts from season to season. In November the cows are pregnant, and the bulls are no longer so watchful. Migrating and winter herds are mixtures of young and old, male and female. In spring, they begin the return migration together. The cows stay in lower valleys and meadows while bulls go higher. While calving, the cows are alone or in twos or threes, but as soon as the calves can run about, they join in larger herds. In September these herds break up in new ways as the bulls return to gather their harems.

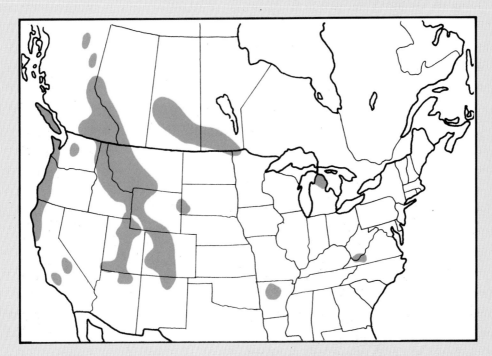

ELK FACTS

Habitat: Rocky Mountain forests and meadows.

Habits: Herd animals; bulls have harems. Feed at dawn and late afternoon.

Food: Varied. Grass and herbs; leaves, buds, bark and young shoots of trees and shrubs. Prefer grass. Aspen and willow.

Size and Weight: Bulls are 7½-9½ feet (2¼-2¾ meters) long; tail ⅝ inches (12-20 centimeters); 4½-5 feet (1.4-1.5 meters) high at shoulder; 600-900 pounds (270-400 kilograms). Cows are three-quarters the size of bulls.

Life Span: Fourteen years in the wild; 25 in captivity.

Locomotion: A graceful run as fast as 35 miles per hour (56 kilometers).

Voice: Calves squeal or bleat; adults have a coarse, explosive bark and a resonant bugling.

Elk have little to fear

A mature elk has few enemies. It can escape them at a speed of 35 miles an hour (55 kilometers) or defend itself with its hooves or antlers. Calves or crippled elk may become prey to bears, coyotes, cougars or wolves. But people are the elk's most dangerous enemies, using land the elk needs.

What Can YOU Do?

The forests of America are faced with many problems. Growing numbers of people need more and more living space and houses in which to live. This means that more and more forests will be cut down to make room for people and to supply wood to build their houses. Because there are only so many trees in America, our forest land is shrinking and wildlife habitats are being destroyed.

What is the solution?

1. Scientists are breeding new "super trees," which grow faster and stronger trees than we now know. This means timber for our housing needs can be produced on fewer acres than would be needed by regular trees.

2. Don't waste tree products. Americans are terribly wasteful and use more paper than most of the rest of the world combined. You can help by discouraging this kind of waste. The next time you go to the grocery store, take a bag with you. Don't depend on the store to give you a bag. Ask the worker at the hamburger stand not to give you paper wrapping, which will just be thrown away. Save newspapers for recycling.

3. Find out how forests are managed. The two biggest managers of our public forests are the U.S. Forest Service and the Bureau of Land Management. Find out where the nearest regional office of either of these agencies is by writing to its Washington, D.C., office. (The Bureau of Land Management is most active in the western states.) Ask for information on how the agency works. You will find that many decisions on how our forests are managed are partly based on open meetings and letters from the public. If you can attend such a meeting, you will learn much about how public forests are managed and how people in your area feel about wildlife.

4. Join a group that works for wildlife. Groups of people can often accomplish much more than one person working alone. If you're in Scouts, suggest a pack or troop project that will help forest wildlife or work to get merit badges or achievement awards for forestry and wildlife conservation. Many 4-H clubs are involved in similar projects. If you belong to a church group, suggest a tree-planting project. Many state conservation agencies are eager to have volunteer help. Some even offer summer work camps to boys and girls interested in helping wildlife.